Contents

Published by Collins
An imprint of HarperCollins*Publishers*
The News Building, 1 London Bridge Street, London, SE1 9GF, UK

HarperCollins*Publishers*
Macken House, 39/40 Mayor Street Upper, Dublin 1, DO1 C9W8, Ireland

Browse the complete Collins catalogue at
www.collins.co.uk

© HarperCollins*Publishers* Limited 2021

10 9 8 7 6 5 4 3

ISBN 978-0-00-846888-0

British Library Cataloguing-in-Publication Data
A catalogue record for this publication is available from the British Library.

Compiled by: Fiona Macgregor
Publisher: Elaine Higgleton
Product manager: Letitia Luff
Commissioning editor: Rachel Houghton
Edited by: Hannah Hirst-Dunton
Editorial management: Oriel Square
Cover designer: Kevin Robbins
Cover illustrations: Jouve India Pvt. Ltd.
Additional text credit: p 3–9 Gill Budgell,
p 10–11, 22–31 Fiona Macgregor p 12–21 Claire Llewellyn
Internal illustrations: p 10–11 Q2Amedia
p 13, 15, 17, 19, 21 Martin Sanders, p 26–31 Sahitya Rani
Typesetter: Jouve India Pvt. Ltd.
Production controller: Lyndsey Rogers
Printed and Bound in the UK using 100% Renewable Electricity at Martins the Printers

Acknowledgements

With thanks to all the kindergarten staff and their schools around the world who have helped with the development of this course, by sharing insights and commenting on and testing sample materials:

Calcutta International School: Sharmila Majumdar, Mrs Pratima Nayar, Preeti Roychoudhury, Tinku Yadav, Lakshmi Khanna, Mousumi Guha, Radhika Dhanuka, Archana Tiwari, Urmita Das; Gateway College (Sri Lanka): Kousala Benedict; Hawar International School: Kareen Barakat, Shahla Mohammed, Jennah Hussain; Manthan International School: Shalini Reddy; Monterey Pre-Primary: Adina Oram; Prometheus School: Aneesha Sahni, Deepa Nanda; Pragyanam School: Monika Sachdev; Rosary Sisters High School: Samar Sabat, Sireen Freij, Hiba Mousa; Solitaire Global School: Devi Nimmagadda; United Charter Schools (UCS): Tabassum Murtaza and staff; Vietnam Australia International School: Holly Simpson

The publishers wish to thank the following for permission to reproduce photographs.

(t = top, c = centre, b = bottom, r = right, l = left)

p 3tl Steve Cukrov/Shutterstock, p 3cl Serhiy Kobyakov/Shutterstock, p 3cr Ursa Studio/Shutterstock, p 3bl Sari Sanee/Shutterstock, p 3br bergamont/Shutterstock, p 3, 4, 5, 7–9 Steve Lumb, p 6, p 9tr Serhiy Kobyakov/Shutterstock, p 12 Corbis/Ecoscene/Ian Beames, p 14 Corbis/Kennan Ward, p 16 Warren Photographic, p 18 Nature Picture Library/Tim Martin, p 20 Alamy/David Boag, p 22–3 Gudrun Muenz/Shutterstock, p 22 Africa Studio/Shutterstock, p 23 Olga_i/Shutterstock, p 24 Vishnevskiy Vasily/Shutterstock, p 25 jps/Shutterstock, p 24–5nasse/Shutterstock

Fruit

apples

bananas

grapes

oranges

melons

strawberries

We like fruit

I like eating apples.

I like eating bananas.

I like eating grapes.

I like eating oranges.

I like eating melon.

We all like eating strawberries.

My house

house

garage

door

The pond

We can see frogs.

We can see snails.

We can see dragonflies.

We can see fish.

We can see a bird.

Growing and changing

baby child adult

foal   horse

egg　　　chick　　　hen

caterpillar

pupa

butterfly

Day and night

Wake up, get up.
Good day, good day.

The sun is up.
It's time to play.

We eat and run
and learn and sing.

The sun shines down
on everything.

Slow down, lie down.
Turn out the light.

The moon is here.
Good night, good night.

Reading notes

Story	Sounds	Language structures
Fruit	'i' 'a' 'l' 'f'	Saying what they like: *I like/ we like*
My house	'm' 'b' 'd'	Talking about houses: *This is my...*
The pond	'w' 'c'	Saying what they can see: *We can see...*
Growing and changing	'm' 'b'	Identifying big and small; saying: *It is a...*
Day and night	'd' 'p'	Using the phrases *It is...* and *In the...*

When you read these stories to your children at home, point out the new sound(s) in each story. Ask: *What sound is this? What letter is this?* Encourage your child to find the letter on the page. Then get them to say the sound, and the word, out loud.

Practise these language structures by asking questions. For example, ask: *What fruit do you like to eat?* to elicit the response: *I like eating (name)*; or ask: *What do we say at bedtime?* to get the answer: *We say good night.*